THE

Fiction

Flying to Nowhere
The Adventures of Speedfall
Tell It Me Again
The Burning Boys
Look Twice
The Worm and the Star
A Skin Diary
The Memoirs of
Laetitia Horsepole
Flawed Angel

Poetry

Fairground Music
The Tree That Walked
Cannibals and Missionaries
Epistles to Several Persons
The Mountain in the Sea
Lies and Secrets
The Illusionists
Waiting for the Music
The Beautiful Inventions
Selected Poems 1954 to 1982
Partingtime Hall
(with James Fenton)
The Grey Among the Green
The Mechanical Body
Stones and Fires
Collected Poems
Now and for a Time
Ghosts
The Space of Joy
Song & Dance

Pebble & I
Writing the Picture
(with David Hurn)
Dream Hunter
(with Nicola LeFanu)
New Selected Poems 1983–2008
The Dice Cup
Gravel in My Shoe

Criticism

The Sonnet
W. H. Auden: a Commentary
Who is Ozymandias? And Other
Puzzles in Poetry

For Children

Herod Do Your Worst
Squeaking Crust
The Spider Monkey Uncle King
The Last Bid
The Extraordinary Wool Mill and
Other Stories
Come Aboard and Sail Away
You're Having Me On

As Editor

The Chatto Book of Love Poetry
The Dramatic Works of John Gay
The Oxford Book of Sonnets
W. H. Auden: Poems Selected by
John Fuller
Alexander Pope: Poems Selected
by John Fuller

THE BONE FLOWERS

or, Blueprints for a Disappearance

John Fuller

John Fuller [signature]

Chatto & Windus
LONDON

Printed in a limited edition of 500 copies

by Chatto & Windus, an imprint of Vintage,
20 Vauxhall Bridge Road,
London SW1V 2SA

Chatto & Windus is part of the Penguin Random House group of companies
whose addresses can be found at global.penguinrandomhouse.com

Copyright © John Fuller 2016

John Fuller has asserted his right to be identified as the author of this
Work in accordance with the Copyright, Designs and Patents Act 1988

First published by Chatto & Windus in 2016

www.vintage-books.co.uk

A CIP catalogue record for this book is available from the British Library

ISBN 9781784741525

Typeset in India by Thomson Digital Pvt Ltd, Noida, Delhi

Printed and bound in Great Britain by TJ International ltd, padstow, Cornwall

Penguin Random House is committed to a sustainable future
for our business, our readers and our planet. This book is made
from Forest Stewardship Council® certified paper.

*For Bernard O'Donoghue and Andrew McNeillie,
with thanks for the SFS*

One

1

When does a poem start? It's hard to say.
    Who cares? It's more or less mysterious.
The notebook says on such and such a day,
    And dedicated scholars make a fuss
Of every small calendrical *donnée*.
    Yet everything that writing means to us
Transcends the scribblings in a poet's journal.
Once the ink dries, the poem is eternal.

2

But still, we need to know the place and time.
    Suspicious of the bliss that ignorance is,
We want to know what triggers the sublime,
    What tips a feeling into utterances,
What turns a rumination into rhyme
    And why. And when. What are the circumstances?
Does Spring or disappointment make it viable?
Is mild ill-health still utterly reliable?

3

Housman thought so, but I disagree.
    Surely the verse you write will be much duller
If you are feeling lousy. Won't it be
    Somehow less colourful if you're off-colour?
(But better not too healthy: we agree
    That no one wants to write in Technicolor.

Better to smoke a lot like Beryl Bainbridge
Than pedal heartily all over Cambridge.)

4

Better to write your best, but for the masses
    (At least a readership like Pope's or Byron's),
Better to don your specs than opera glasses.
    Better to potter safely the environs,
Than stagger to the peak, of Mount Parnassus,
    Listen to human voices, not the Sirens',
For their seductive babble seems to say
That sense in poetry is *démodé*.

5

I took a journey, the Cross Country line,
    Thus energetically named to show
What joy it is to race up England's spine
    Through famous cities that you barely know
To give a reading at Newcastle-upon-Tyne.
    It seemed a large, symbolic way to go:
Oxford, Birmingham, and then a fork
To the North-East, Derby, Doncaster and York.

6

York was the birthplace of Great Uncle Wiz,
    Largest of modern poets, and the one
Who married metrical exigencies
    With ordered thinking and a sense of fun,
Who knew what love demands, what evil is
    And all that timeliness depends upon,
And how, when you're by far the youngest brother,
The audience you play to is your mother.

7

(And by the way, if ever a day went by
    Without producing verse, he felt quite ill,
And unlike some he didn't justify
    His status as a poet with some shrill
Assertion of insanity, or try
    To kill himself. Keeping alert but still,
He managed to write great poems with the best of them,
And of a kind much saner than the rest of them.)

8

This is the county of my origins,
    Well-butter-toasted Yorkshire, ignorant
Either of my achievements or my sins.
    I recognise, a passing revenant,
The landscape where my brief blood-line begins,
    My great-grandfather's grandfathers (I can't
Go further back than this, all faceless myths,
These timber-merchant Norths and grocer Smiths).

9

The journey was much like the way we live,
    Attended by anxiety and dread,
The management of bureaucrat and spiv,
    Transport of souls, half living and half dead,
The sense of waste, and no one to forgive,
    Trapped in a limbo like a watershed
Where you have left, or will never see, your friends,
In fractured systems, milked for dividends.

I saw some notably run-down locales:
　　Dead stacks of damaged cars, the Rose and Crown,
Wet yards with shattered pallets, grey canals
　　Where coloured boats, half-hidden, floated down
The routes that England cut for minerals,
　　The ugly make-do of the out-of-town,
The backs of semis rawly extemporised,
Like life itself, its anguish undisguised.

I saw a hiker looking for a linnet.
　　I saw a briefcase looking for the Gents.
I saw a chapel with a billboard (in it
　　There was a waiting-room for penitents,
With trains for heaven leaving every minute).
　　I saw a factory for armaments
And sheds for windows with no windows in them,
And ads for prizes, though no one would win them.

I saw an orange football, half-deflated,
　　Lost in a spinney, like a silent wail.
I saw a crossing where a cyclist waited
　　As though a world of shadowy lanes and ale
Was just about to be inaugurated.
　　Herb Robert sprouted by a rusty rail.
A world where trivial pleasures fail to please
And disappointment spreads like a disease.

13

And then the train pulled into Darlington:
    Three great arches, ironwork that spanned
The vaulting with six-pointed stars, and on
    The platform tall Corinthian columns and
Silvery railings. Ian Hamilton
    Must have thought the station much too grand
When first he left the city of his youth
To go to Oxford in pursuit of truth.

14

The order of these northern cities wouldn't
    Be something I'd expect to lay a claim to.
Typical ignorant southerner, I shouldn't
    Wonder, is what you'd say. I wouldn't aim to,
Though. I couldn't even name them, couldn't
    Recognise them – not until I came to
Golden Durham, ecclesiastically
Privileged above its peaceful valley.

15

While we are there, let's make a pause
    To say what most of this is all about,
Or hopes to be. One must be clear, because
    So much of poetry is out-and-out
Mystification, with no get-out clause.
    You have to sit and hear the poet spout,
Transfixed by gestures, and his manic glint
(Though aren't we glad that they invented print).

Print may be turned back to, but you're perplexed
    When listening to John Ashbery or Homer.
(Print can't be trusted, though. Predictive text
    Labels this very stanza 'Ottawa Roma'.
I wonder what it might come up with next
    In its presumptuous call for a misnomer?
Metrical theory is already tortuous
Without 'amphibians', 'ises', 'snaps' and 'torches'.)

    17

I'd like to tell you where all this is leading,
    Explain what happened when I ventured forth
One day in Spring to give a poetry reading.
    Too many hours it took: after the fourth,
With all that dingy scenery receding,
    I'd sooner have been headed not just to t' North
But to New Zealand or the Caribbean.
And then, in Darlington, I thought of Ian.

    18

And later, in my Newcastle hotel,
    I thought of him, at dead of night among
The sounds of pleasure-leaving cars and well-
    Oiled fans and clubbers. Below my window, young
Women (Where were they going? Who could tell?)
    Tottered on high heels very slowly, clung
To each other, shrieking, as though blindfold,
With naked shoulders, impervious to cold.

19

What had they been drinking? Newcastle Brown?
  Or Jägerbombs? Or various kinds of dope?
The liquid that most easily slips down
  Is that Rhône nectar, Newcastle of the Pope,
With its deep purple, ageing into brown
  (Which you will think a paradox, I hope,
Since I have doubled up a rhyme and cheated,
And have no inclination to delete it).

20

Four a.m.! In this great northern city
  Which once had dealings with coal, steel and iron,
And now is known for poetry! A pity.
  But still, to Pat and Keith, and Sean O'Brien,
And all enthusiasts on the committee,
  I owe a lot. It's just that, oh Daughters of Zion,
Why such little clothing and self-control
In this deep April dark night of the soul?

21

Four a.m.! *Bêtiserie* I might
  Have shared with Ian, fit for his cynic's ears,
That this would have been my audience tonight
  If culture didn't move in different spheres.
He would have muttered something impolite,
  But he's been dead for the last thirteen years
(Thirteen empty years since last he spoke!)
And death itself has made its own grim joke.

22

Four a.m.! The hour when the Destroyer
    Shows you the blue-prints for your disappearance
(Appropriate, since time is his employer).
    You'll notice that their style is incoherence,
Facteur Cheval rather than Powell and Moya.
    Planning, perhaps, may never give them clearance,
And if you make a strenuous objection,
You're hoping for a permanent rejection.

23

Four a.m.! I should have had a brandy,
    Though brandy sometimes keeps you from your zizz:
It's dandy if you're feeling jack-a-dandy,
    But jolts you out of slumber. As it is,
A paracetamol would come in handy,
    Or Alka Seltzer with its soothing fizz.
Bloody Newcastle! The hours they keep!
Everyone's seventeen! They never sleep!

24

Four a.m.! People were going home,
    Vodka and consciousness almost extinct,
My woken brain a seething honeycomb
    Of buzzing thoughts. Closing the curtains, I blinked:
My room lay crouched in deadly monochrome.
    I knew I couldn't get to sleep. I winked
Well enough, but never reached the fortieth,
Pondering the injustices of death.

25

Whenever it is, it always seems too soon.
    Ian at 63 had more than most,
Shakespeare's was certainly inopportune
    At 52. Lawrence became a ghost
At 47. Byron? In bed by noon
    At 36. They blasted the Last Post
For Owen at the age of 24.
(But Yeats at 73 still wanted more.)

26

Who wouldn't? Not all deaths are long, or gory,
    But simply drawing up your balance sheet
Is all finality and little glory.
    Whatever the sum, it seems like a defeat.
You're being written out of your own story,
    When not much can be said to be complete.
Imagine: a line of fine hypothesis
Boldly begins, then simply ends, – like this.

27

As though you launched some deathless words into
    The fragile air, and wind blew them away.
Such as: 'Season of mists and mellow frui—'
    And then: 'The woods decay, the woods decay—'
Or perhaps: 'Let me not to the marriage of true—'
    And: 'When I have fears that I may—' And then: 'Say—'.
Even the most sublime of our creations
Succumb to the Destroyer's impatience.

He'll give the signs. You're ashen for a smoke
    And feel your pockets for your fags. 'Ahem!'
He mutters at your shoulder. 'Do you want to choke
    On your own blood? I'll see you at the Crem . . .'
But no one thinks their coffin is bespoke,
    Even when dreaming their own requiem.
We can imagine immortality
Easily – but never ceasing to be.

29

And if we do? Why, then, perhaps we're Keats,
    The poet of painful contrasts. In the room,
All warmth and kisses, fever and sweetmeats;
    Outside, the chill Destroyer who'd consume
Him long before he could complete the feats
    He had in mind. How personal is doom?
We are in awe of those we live among
Whom the gods love, indeed, and will die young.

30

To have no hope of your inamorata,
    Nor any of those dark-eyed signorinas
At the age of 25! To be a martyr
    To suffocation! To say farewell to Venus
Among the beauties of the Scalinata
    Di Trinità dei Monti! To see Silenus
Grinning from your fire-place at eye-level
Through the long hours of pain, a retching devil!

31

They took his mask in death, as they were used
    To do (physiognomical tableaux
For curious devotees, who thus abused
    The memory). However, I suppose
He'd had the life mask done, looking amused
    And breathing with a straw stuck in his nose.
I've got a cast of it upon my wall.
It doesn't feel like stalking him at all.

32

Rather, it makes him seem a living being,
    The face that launched a thousand lines, the real
Keats. But I can sense you disagreeing.
    That veritable nose and chin reveal
Nothing, you say, and those blank eyes, unseeing,
    Have little to do with the Keatsian ideal.
For sure, he saw that sparrow on his sill,
But ordinary sparrows peck there still.

33

Who is to say that Keats's painful parting
    Was any worse than mine or yours might be?
We live with our mistakes, forever smarting
    Under rebukes and put-downs, foolishly
Regretting things we did, forever starting
    Projects of futile possibility
And, as our literary hopes diminish,
Planning the epics we will never finish.

34

All that matters is what we leave behind
    That turns into the future, not the past.
Knowing we die is nothing we should mind.
    Lessons we learn from life are what must last
So that life everywhere can be designed,
    An endless play, and we the changing cast.
Human self-consciousness will never stop,
Ambiguous as that fable by Aesop.

35

Theories about experience allow
    A lawful longing for those painted grapes.
Remember Browning's young grammarian, how
    He uttered smugly: 'Leave Now for dogs and apes!
Man has Forever!' And yet we live the Now!
    Despite our language's ephemeral shapes,
A word reminds us what we ought to feel.
Our language is the menu, not the meal.

Two

1

And now, I think, it's time to start the story.
    A poem needs one if it's to come alive.
The poet's circumstances are a bore, he
    Shouldn't express opinions or contrive
Jokes that are private or inflammatory.
    A poem's fiction. It needs narrative drive.
You mustn't think of it as artifice.
In any case, I need to tell you this:

2

Can you imagine someone who is so rich
    That he believes he can forestall his death?
Whose need for millions is a constant itch?
    Camels and needles come to mind (as saith
The scripture, with much other warning which
    We ought to take to heart, while we have breath –
But which of course none of us ever do,
Now that we know that scripture isn't true).

3

Young Billy Emerald was left a pile
    At an unusually early age.
His grandfather was something mercantile
    And liked young Billy. To his cousins' rage,
And to the detriment of their life-style,
    The money went to Billy at a stage

When all that he was interested in
Were puzzles, toys and games, and how to win.

4

From infancy he had preferred success
    In laying out and managing his toys
To any sort of motherly caress.
    He liked to paint, made very little noise,
Passed his exams with credit – nonetheless
    Was not unpopular with other boys:
Later at Oxford was the cuddliest cub
To be detrousered at the Dining Club.

5

He was an aesthete, sure enough, but cash
    Was interesting too. What it could do
To multiply itself with great panache
    It seemed to do with ease. It grew and grew
Until it bloomed, a quite enormous stash,
    And he was rich, not merely well-to-do.
Then, at the age of twenty-one, the Trust
Came into his possession, as it must.

6

Fast forward through his years in high finance.
    Fast forward through the heady time he spent
Leading the art world in a pretty dance
    Of secret dealings not quite fraudulent
Nor honest, either, years of elegance
    And acquisition, fat years when he went
Through several marriages and several dowries
That helped him to invest in Moores and Lowries.

14

7

He was an opportunist. Of the market
    He liked to say when risking an ascription:
'It isn't just the Porsche but where you park it.'
    With just the slightest of a tweaked inscription
And flattering cultivation of his target,
    He could sell ancient relics to Egyptian
Museums that were their own, and furthermore
Had just been stolen from them months before.

8

He floated many schemes on unsuspecting
    Members of the public ignorant
Of all the niceties of art collecting,
    Greedy for bargains, and so tolerant
They'd never dream of asking or objecting.
    Provenance? No, no, irrelevant!
Prints by Picasso? Immediate possession!
(No mention of the size of the impression.)

9

He floated schemes, he floated in his dreams:
    Using your charm like this to muddle others
About the different roles of Is and Seems
    Is easy for those who did it to their mothers.
It's one of life's most serviceable memes.
    It's why the will conveniently smothers
All virtue, though it knows it to be true:
Your own Othello's doing it to *you*.

And yet he really did believe in choice
    Enabling the created life, that beauty
To which all wealth eventually gives voice.
    From trivial alternatives (the duty
To ditch a Ford in favour of Rolls-Royce,
    Or Vernon Handley for Ricardo Muti)
To choices of immense significance,
Like only refusing a Birthday Honour once.

Lord Emerald, as lastly he became,
    Was much the most complaisant of his peers,
Sought for the glowing credence of his name
    Not for the brilliance between his ears;
Sought, not for quality, but for acclaim,
    By galleries, museums, auctioneers,
By colleges and other institutions
Who valued, not ideas, but contributions.

His genial profile nodded on committees.
    He spoke on panels with a playful smile.
He'd say he thought it was a thousand pities
    That painters did not feel it was worthwhile
Pleasing the public. However in the City's
    Eager boardrooms he could reconcile
Such populism with an eagerness
To sell them blank or dribbled canvases.

13

And in his own collections the wild daemon
    Of *je m'en fous* was slowly gathering
Friezes of nappies, heads of blood or semen,
    Installations made of fat and string,
The juvenilia of Tracey Emin
    (Not vastly different from the real thing)...
This is the region of the opportune,
Where rainy day negotiates blue moon.

14

He didn't actually *like* them, but
    He knew which side his bread was buttered. Taste
Can be thrusting, cut-and-thrust, if not clear-cut.
    These at a subtle moment could be placed
On public sale. The case was open-and-shut:
    Purchase at leisure and resell in haste.
So long as he could make a healthy profit,
He looked for novelty and plenty of it.

15

But those who knew him knew what pleased him best:
    Murano glass, views of the Grand Canal,
A cinquecento inlaid walnut chest,
    Early bibles, the original
Drafts of 'Dulce et Decorum Est',
    Miniature models of the Taj Mahal
And other intricacies, toothpicks, netsuke,
And violins he loaned to Sitkovetsky.

Conservative, you say? He was a Tory
    After all. He jockeyed and caballed
Like any other. But though his head was hoary,
    And choleric, and bulbous, and thick-skulled,
You'll recollect the opening of this story:
    He still was little Billy Emerald,
And eminence not what he was expecting.
All he enjoyed was playing and collecting.

Enjoyed? That fatal hope in life? Uniqueness
    That our self-consciousness is cruelly born to?
There is a force within us, drawn to bleakness
    Though we may be, that's fortunately sworn to
Make joy of it, and know it. It's our weakness.
    And where we cannot celebrate, we mourn, too.
And wait for the Destroyer of Enjoyment
(Who's always near, for that is his employment).

For Billy, the simple spirit who survived
    Inside Lord Emerald, still hopeful of
Joys of the body, though for long miswived,
    Still hopeful, surely, of some sort of love,
That moment had with certainty arrived
    When Christians used to start to think above
This world, and others at least, faced with its ills,
Called in their lawyers and made their wills.

He stared one night, appalled, into the mirror
    In the shower-room of his flat off Piccadilly.
'My God, what's this?' he gasped, and then leaned nearer.
    'It isn't me! This doesn't look like Billy!'
He pulled one eye-pouch down. Couldn't be clearer:
    Someone was in his skin. He screamed quite shrilly,
For in that fatal second he had lost a
Face so long familiar, to an impostor.

20

It was, you see, the face of the Destroyer.
    After a while you see it everywhere:
A wrinkle calculated to annoy; a
    Mole that wasn't there before (with hair);
A nose like a disaster out of Goya;
    Skin like the surface of a Camembert.
It's yours, of course, this dissipated phiz.
It's everyone's at last, and it was his.

21

He couldn't sleep. He couldn't even try to,
    For sleep is a great gift, not an endeavour.
Sleep is a society you sigh to
    Join, though someone blackballs you whenever
Your name crops up. It's an island you can't fly to,
    Where in your dreams you know you'll live for ever.
Solving that conundrum's self-defeating,
Like betting you won't win a prize. Or cheating.

Life lay in tatters in his buzzing mind:
    His second wife, an object of suspicion;
The children that he'd had to leave behind
    Who only visited with her permission;
That once upon a time he'd been resigned
    To never seeing at all; the bleak tradition
Of walking glumly on a wind-swept isthmus
In Wales, with his first wife, every other Christmas.

Ah, Judy, Judy, was he such a pain?
    You grew impatient. You began to doubt him.
He only seemed to live inside his brain.
    You always needed to know more about him,
And never did. This drove you quite insane,
    Till you decided you could do without him
And cast him off. So sad, so bittersweet,
That after everything you longed to meet.

The things we have are never quite enough.
    We scrutinise them fiercely for perfection.
In marriage if you tug at one handcuff
    You'll find the other tugs back. Disaffection
Is just a kind of fraying at the edges, rough
    In every sense. In Judy's recollection
Every advance pushed Billy further back.
Yet still she had this instinct for attack.

25

But in their greying afterlife, without
    His silence or her constant need to know,
Their early flame survived the winds of doubt.
    She was quite happy in her studio,
Selling her pots and slowly growing stout.
    Their difficulties seemed so long ago.
They sometimes shared a weekend in Llandovery,
In peaceful deference and real discovery.

26

Pathetic, really. Life was such a mess
    In all respects save only the aesthetic.
Surviving relationships were passionless,
    His crushes calculated and synthetic.
Not that this put him under any stress,
    Since hopes of that sort were, he knew, pathetic.
He was much happier simply being Billy,
In his lavish bachelor flat off Piccadilly.

27

Happy with Heidsieck at an exhibition
    With he himself the object of attention,
Happy when reading that an unknown Titian
    Was saved for the nation through his intervention,
Happy when bidding for a first edition
    While letting it be known that his intention
Was simply the perverse one (such a devil!)
Of getting the price up to a certain level.

28

We're all of us nearer death at four a.m.,
    When most removed from all the furniture
Of our created lives. The requiem
    Our mind constructs, and the creased sepulchre
We lie in, conspire against us and we make of them
    A wakefulness that holds us prisoner,
Prone to the mercy of our biorhythms,
Rehearsing sheep, strong verbs or logarithms.

29

Let's leave him now. For dawn, that repossesses
    The night's tormented body and its ache,
Will soon be here. His clock's three little SSS's
    Show it to be five fifty-five. He'll wake
To that reliable pale light that blesses
    The sinner, forgives each terrible mistake
And leaves him, though sleepless, readier to face
Another day. Let's give the man some space.

Three

1

The power of music is unarguable
    When we remember it, or when it's playing.
It's what it's written on that is the trouble.
    What is all that mediaeval vellum saying?
Unreadable notation in the rubble
    Of long-extinguished cities is dismaying.
(I had a colleague who was working on
The unheard scores of ancient Babylon.)

2

My 78s are awfully out of shape
    However fine the gold-and-chocolate label.
My LPs are shot through with sapphire-scrape,
    And anyway, who's kept their old turn-table?
A tape-recorder tends to stretch the tape
    So that it warbles. Now I am unable
To access 'tracks' I saved on Spotify.
My CDs, I am told, will shortly die.

3

The Babylonians, like us, could hear
    The well-known songs that meant the most to them
Continually, in their inner ear.
    This is the mind's resourceful stratagem
For hoarding music's healing atmosphere,
    And every note of melody's a gem

That radiates, within our unforgetting,
The strange and unique beauty of its setting.

4

These riches, though, because they are alive
    Are also at his mercy. Populations
Connected in their head by swing and jive
    Or by a stately theme-and-variations
Have always somehow managed to contrive
    A mystical unity, like congregations
Singing hymns. But these, too, have to die.
And so does music in their memory.

5

Cheap, as Coward said, but in its way
    The dearest thing we have. And he may scoff,
The Enemy of Joy. He need not say
    A thing. He gives a deprecating cough
Silently at your shoulder. That's his way.
    He listens for a while, then turns it off,
All that was in your head – My Dear Old Swanee,
Mahler's Fourth, Dire Straits or *Mahagonny*.

6

Strange, these resources of the mind: the germ
    Of melody acquired in babyhood,
Rocked on the breast, and then we reaffirm
    In our inner ear all that we've understood.
Irrational attachment, in an ear-worm
    That tells us the music's got into our blood.
It's there as we brush our teeth. It's in our head
At four a.m. And when we get out of bed.

7

For one whole summer I could hear Ravel
    Throughout the night from Gers to the Cevennes.
Mostly it was the Piano Trio fell
    Into my head like some fine specimen
Of heaven overheard. I couldn't tell
    How it got there. It came again and again.
And when that was exhausted, then began
His magic opera, concerto and pavane.

8

A whip sends fingers to create events
    Improbably upon the ivory.
Idylls of quavers are rich implements
    Of joy, or ennui begetting cruelty.
The clock complains, the wallpaper laments,
    A blue note sounds in the chinoiserie.
To thunder to a climax is to live!
And the wounded creature will at last forgive.

9

But music deploys no tenses. It exists
    Afresh inside the heads of those who hear
Either the thunder of the pianist's
    Descending octaves or the patient, clear
Pianissimo of levelled wrists
    That arch above the keys, or even mere
Silence – that useful space around a note
That shapes a sound by being its antidote.

10

It does instil nostalgia: from the page
    The scribbled ink creates the sweetest face,
Dancing for ever on her courtly stage
    Where all is immanence, reflective grace
And the defunctive tempo of *cortège*.
    Where loss is beauty at its slowest pace,
As though the point was never to have been
(Though told of it from birth) a future queen.

11

But You-Know-Who will come to take them all,
    Our ears and understanding finally
Defeated, silence standing like a wall
    Or locked into notation's vacancy.
And the bow-tied composer will let fall
    His baton, once his surrogates are free,
The naughty Enfant who exclaimed 'Maman!'
The pacing rapt Infante, now long gone.

12

And His own deathly music is the drum,
    Playful and insistent (think Steve Reich).
Elastic balance of the wrist and thumb
    Makes every bouncing stroke a look-alike,
Although percussion's strict harmonium
    Advances and delays the time to strike
So that a kind of doubt remains throughout
Which of the drums is milliseconds out.

13

Expecting time to be a clock that ticks,
  Your brain will trip and skitter on his traps.
For every four, your frightened pulse beats six.
  You process weird ectopic flams and taps.
You're hunched above your flickering ruffs and licks
  And scatter rat-a-plans in rattled raps.
You're terrified by all this tarradiddle
And punch-drunk with his drummer's paradiddle.

14

You feel him when your heart begins to thud.
  He grins insanely at asynchrony.
A valve plops open like a frog in mud
  And he rejoices in such syncope
That means he has his fingers in your blood,
  Dabbling and drumming interferingly,
Making your body dance: tattoos, galops,
Fox-trots and jitterbugs – and then it stops.

15

Now all of this is just by way of saying
  That when, the following week, Lord Emerald
Found himself somewhere west of Wessex staying
  With Lady Sliphanger at Witts End (called
'A little gem' by Pevsner) there was playing
  Remembered music in his head. Ripe swelled
The strings of Handel, over and over, all
The relished pomp of the Dead March from *Saul*.

16

Perhaps it calmed him after his long night
    Of jitters, as music does in times of stress.
It woke with him in his four-poster, light
    Streaming behind the curtains. You may guess
What tune he hummed, descending to reunite
    At breakfast with the Dowager Countess
(Who thought of any singing as quite jolly,
Rather the opposite of melancholy).

17

Handel, indeed, and scrambled egg and bacon,
    A linen napkin and the *Telegraph*,
Are just the thing for us when we awaken
    (Smiling at the late Earl's better half)
And a second cup of coffee has been taken
    (Or rather poured, by one of her silent staff).
Surely (he thought) we trust these moments to arrive
When once again it's good to be alive.

18

A charming little thing of 83
    She was, with hair like Piaf or Colette
And eyes enlarged with curiosity.
    One hand made circles with a cigarette
While the other picked her lips for its debris.
    She thought it very strange to be in debt.
Pushing her plate aside, she blew out smoke
And pressed the stub out in the cooling yolk.

19

Their conversation of the night before
    Was now resumed with more decisiveness,
Though there were many aspects to explore.
    To put it simply, the Dowager Countess
Owed much in taxes, had no cash, therefore
    Proposed to sell some manuscripts, unless
The Government were willing to agree
To take them for the British Library.

20

Or rather, she wasn't eager to forgo
    The millions of dollars she might get
(Or yen, if the buyers came from Tokyo)
    At public auction. It was quite a threat,
And Emerald proposed this quid pro quo,
    Whereby the nation never would forget
The Earl's illustrious name, forever linked
With deathless manuscripts by Shakespeare inked.

21

Not Shakespeare's holograph, you understand,
    Simply some ancestor of the dead Earl's
Who copied sonnets in his own crabbed hand
    And hid them in a chest with gold and pearls.
The texts were hard to read and rarely scanned
    Over the centuries, all blots and twirls,
And two unclear initials, but unsigned
(Besides, the secret drawer was hard to find).

22

The Seventh Earl had found them, to be sure.
    The two initials surely were of the Second,
And in the absence of a signature,
    A loyalty to family (he reckoned)
Trumped their significance to literature.
    And though Bardolators and guineas beckoned,
He fully resisted their intense campaign
And put them in the secret drawer again.

23

'In lieu of taxes.' A delightful phrase,
    That strikes with eager hope the desperate hearts
Of any distraught heirs obliged to raise
    Large sums. Their number-crunching counterparts
At HMRC, happy nowadays
    To take (when Government funding of the arts
Stands at an all-time low), make contributions
Which cost them nothing, to national institutions.

24

'In lieu' implies some sort of diminution:
    Instead of substance, all you get is shadow,
Provisional thinking rather than solution,
    No actual poem but a month at Yaddo,
No blinding truth but blind circumlocution.
    The understudy is an eager saddo.
The stand-in can't do anything but stand.
We'd never choose to eat the cheaper brand.

'In lieu' can be positive, of course,
    The province of any moral storyteller.
How better to thwart unnatural intercourse
    Like Angelo's designs on Isabella,
Or Almaviva's on Susanna? Force
    Is demoralising. Why compel her?
The rake who toys with any passing beauty
Has to be tricked, and made to do his duty.

'In lieu of taxes' is a trick of sorts
    To turn an obligation on its head.
It's natural, when the Revenue extorts
    Its share, to feel that it's unwarranted.
What can you do? Try going to the courts?
    It's better to negotiate instead.
'I'm in a dire financial situation,
But there are *these* that I can give the nation.'

And thus it was with Sliphanger's estate,
    The trick, as it quite often is, two-sided.
It needed Emerald to mediate.
    Say, if the Countess were to have decided
That it would suit her to depatriate
    These manuscripts? How terribly misguided!
And further, though the sum were truly stellar,
There'd be no export licence, he would tell her.

And what about the things themselves? Might he . . ?
   Would it be too much trouble? Just a glance?
She rang a bell to call her secretary
   Who crept out from the shadows almost at once,
Clutching a folder with precautionary
   Cotton gloves. He did a little dance
And then with a silent conjuror's a-ha!
Laid down the folder on an escritoire.

Emerald had to wear some gloves as well,
   Since toast and marmalade cannot be trusted
Nor other pots upon the carousel
   Like medlar jelly, Marmite, Dijon mustard,
Not to transmit themselves, by smear or smell,
   So that the precious papers get encrusted.
The secretary bowed, apologised,
But Emerald was not at all surprised.

Turning the papers with their faded ink,
   He felt the deathless words invade his brain,
And as he read the lines they made him think,
   Yet still behind each argued quatorzaine
There ran this silent music like a kink
   Of consciousness, though of a merrier strain
Than *Saul*. It was a bit like 'Ach, du lieber . . .'
Or 'The Arrival of the Queen of Sheba'.

Shall I then say that Eos cared for me,
Whitened my single window euery day

And with her beames lighted my poetry,
And willed the Terrors of the night away?
Heroes who fight long houres to earn their name
May claim a prompt inuigorating bed,
But those whose laboures seek a gradual fame
Despaire of joy vntil the night has fled,
When reason may resume, and the mind greet
The office of the sophist or the bard.
Thought is for them a solitarie feate.
The night is long, and all its minutes hard.
 Much more, then, am I welcome at her feast,
 One who from Night was drawn into her East.

It is an Ethiopian maid who sings.
I hear and write down all her rhapsodies.
Yet after night's delightes, the morning brings
Loue's urgent whispers to his weeping knees.
I haue no passion now, if truth be told.
The light rebukes me. Dewe is on the lawn.
I wished to liue, but neuer to be old.
I am a shape abandoned by the Dawn.
O daughter of Hyperion, make clear
The dying of our nights, and of our daies.
Wake all the worlde, and travel far from here,
Far from an old man's bed and fruitlesse gaze.
 Let boys smile curses from their sweated sheetes,
 And tell the gods how much my heart still beates.

I saw a creature hanging from a stemme,
Another leaping to a bending flow'r,
And had a quainte desire to be like them,
Without all knowledge of the changing hour,

33

Of the abrupt and euer-closing door
Of fatal illness, and aduance of rust,
Of the opposing army's sudden roar
At someone's darling lying in the dust.
Ah, Memnon, whom the tall Achilles slew,
That euer son should fall before his sire!
Now cloudes of starlings stirring in the blue,
Yearly recall smoke rising from his pyre.
   And I am forced to watch each feathered ember
   Mock, in its play, the babe that I remember.

Between my naturall disbelief in death
And knowledge that the world itselfe will cease:
Between the daring capture of a breath
And the large-minded risk of its release,
Stands my vncertain immortalite,
That steadie passage of the pretious air
Which is the gratefull planet's guarranty
Of ready and perpetuall repaire,
Breath after breath released in the conuiction
That my best future lies in the endeuour
To bide my time and to maintain the fiction
That in this moment I might liue for euer,
   Not in the accumulated past,
   But in each latest breath, not yet the last.

How may the gods take back the giftes they make?
It is the pleasure of rewardes to be
More for these giuers, than receiuers, sake,
Their miracles, their magnanimitie,
And for their tender care of all that dies,

And for their passing enuie of mere mortalls.
They moue in state across the changeless skies
To chase Time's wildings from their marble portals,
They grant men's mindeless wishes with a sigh,
They woo the beautie that they never had,
Which is short-liued, but tenderer thereby,
They clutche their hearts and know that they are sad.
   My cricket, tumbling from his blade of grass,
   Sings merrily of all that comes to pass.

W. S.

31

Nothing at all like Shakespeare, you will say?
   It's somehow lacking the authentic spark?
A cynic would suspect there'd been foul play:
   Not enough checking of the watermark,
And wouldn't chemical analysis betray
   A modern ink? There isn't any Dark
Lady or Handsome Youth. The verse is thin
And awkward. No, they can't be genuine.

32

Shakespeareans gathered in the *TLS*
   Like drunkards in a public square: nit-pickers
Pro and con, those eager to digress
   Or savage those they thought had got their knickers
In a twist. But who could really know unless
   There'd been a final word from Brian Vickers?
Or heard the quiet authoritative tones
Of Kerrigan, or Katherine Duncan-Jones?

33

No one would ever come to a conclusion
  Or one that might be deemed to be official.
Now, 'W. S.' was surely an illusion?
  Perhaps it was 'M. E.' Neither initial
Was clear. And each Ovidian allusion
  Was thought either authentic or artificial.
Had Coleridge seen the manuscript and paid
A tribute with his 'Abyssinian' maid?

34

Emerald himself was sole begetter
  Of this great coup, and he was highly praised
For all he'd done (and who could do it better?).
  The Board of the British Library was amazed
('A tricky task, completed to the letter').
  Another million needed to be raised
By Gift Aid, but this was easily adjusted.
Emerald was a trustee to be trusted.

35

But when the fire dies down the room grows chilly.
  The heel-taps flatten after the reception.
Gilding can't halt the festering of the lily.
  The thing begins to feel like a misconception.
The actors forget their parts, and so with Billy.
  Even some unknown Shakespeare's no exception
To the rule that every dazzling fairy tale
Soon, with familiarity, grows stale.

36

Life itself is a wonderful endeavour.
    It seems as unassailable as gold.
But life's a fragile thread that time must sever,
    And our futurity is put on hold.
We all would wish that we could live for ever
    If so we could, – though never being old
(That sentiment was well-expressed by Swift).
But no: life is a loan and not a gift.

37

To outwit death is sometimes a kind of theft.
    Our blood flows to its *terminus ad quem.*
Our rock of being finally is cleft
    And when we approach that hour of four a.m.
Only our crowding memories are left
    And nothing much that can be done with them,
For Billy now that moment was much nearer,
Since first Death watched him from his bathroom mirror.

Four

1

Superstition is the blank relief
    That we can trust ourselves to tell a story
In which we have no credible belief.
    It is the flag-salute without the glory.
It is the trust in tears without real grief.
    Quite simply a mistaken category,
Like fashioning a poem out of jargon,
Or bargaining to get out of a bargain.

2

We do it all the time, out of suspicion
    That we can know the future in advance
If we can strike a deal with it, a mission
    To lead our enemy a merry dance.
'If I have one slight medical condition
    And bravely face it, then there's every chance
I can't acquire another' is the sort
Of thing – illogical (but it's a thought).

3

And there are worse: 'Cutting my fingernails
    Regularly means I'll live for ever.'
'I can't gain weight if I don't get on the scales.'
    'Better never to say "Never say never".'
'I shall feel calmer when I get to Wales.'
    Equivocation isn't very clever.

It tends to minimise an obvious truth
Nothing you do can give you back your youth.

4

Long before that you've played the game of time
    Against him. Soon as you're born, the pack's unpacked
And shuffled. Time itself's the paradigm:
    Fifty-two cards, fifty-two weeks – a fact!
Four suits, four seasons: it's a ludic chime
    That should have told you that the cards are stacked
Against you. What you're dealt is not the same
As what you have to play, a losing game.

5

Season succeeding season, year on year.
    The values shift, and time adjusts its pace.
At first, as eager as a volunteer,
    You play your hand, a King, a Queen, an Ace!
The tricks are easy, and you persevere,
    For time is what you win. It's not a race.
You glow in triumph. Everything is play.
A year is telescoped into a day.

6

But soon you find that time accelerates,
    Like games of poker that go on all night,
Hand after hand, despairing of pairs or straights,
    The betting dull, shades drawn against the light.
Time is like this. The world that fascinates
    Has much to offer to the neophyte,
Then repetition makes him restless, days
That once were idylls turn to tearaways.

7

This is the obscurest of the sorrows,
    Though some say it's entirely an illusion,
That time must be a constant (our tomorrows
    Arriving by the clock, and in profusion),
That time is bound to pay back what it borrows,
    Adjusting fast with slow, and in conclusion
We should take heart, adjust our hopes, and be
Prepared to understand zenosyne.

8

Playing at chess is one way to appease
    The enemy of joy. There is no deal.
The odds are even, though he wins with ease.
    Yet while you play, as in *The Seventh Seal*,
All is not lost, and Mephistopheles
    Is bound by bond to humour your ordeal,
While brilliant combinations mitigate
The speed of his inevitable mate.

9

The answer is a riddle, to be candid.
    Handling the time that's left, that is the trick.
It has to be conceptually expanded.
    You have to be a valiant heretic
Of time's brute orthodoxy, single-handed
    Step from its narrow path, and double-quick
Upend the stupid beast with stumbling-blocks
And thrust him with the sword of paradox.

The self we were is not the self we are.
    The self we are is not the self we will be.
The hopes and habits change, dissimilar
    As astrakhan-with-flaps and snap-brimmed trilby.
We could be either Yogi or Commissar,
    Perhaps not Kim Jong-un, but yes, Kim Philby.
We even deceive ourselves. Our motives change.
We've no idea why what we do feels strange.

11

Of course we want to realise our worth.
    It may be almost hopeless, but worth trying.
We don't know who we are. Our time on earth
    Is short enough to make it terrifying.
We're not the person that we were at birth.
    We're not the person that we will be, dying.
The quick-change artist in his suit of brown
(Ta-dah!) swirls in a crimson evening gown.

12

But there's an upside to these differences
    That in most other ways might seem dismaying.
When finally we realise it is
    The time when our body feels like disobeying
And all the comfortable things it says
    To us, we find with horror it's not saying,
We will not be the same as we are now.
Our present selves will have escaped somehow.

13

The many little selves, from lunch to tea,
    That we procrastinate with (as Macbeth
Declared, tomorrow and tomorrow) we
    Assume as frequently as we take breath.
Who knows what different personality
    I will have adopted at my time of death?
I feel for him enormous sympathy,
But whoever it is, it won't, I think, be me.

14

Modes of existence come and go. They melt
    The one into the other. States of mind
Depend upon the hand that you've been dealt:
    Quite likely that tomorrow you will find
All the anxieties you might have felt
    Played out like cards you will have left behind,
Trumped on the baize. As always, you begin
Again. The next trick is the one to win.

15

In poets you observe the difference:
    The moody Tennyson becoming proud
Of his political magniloquence.
    Wordsworth embracing all he disavowed.
Pound getting desperate to make less sense.
    Donne at the theatre; Donne in his shroud.
Their personalities not only change
But sometimes cover a surprising range.

16

So when the Destroyer leaves his calling card
    Unconscionably early, don't you think
Things might have gone quite differently? Not hard
    To see Sir Wilfred Owen, the worse for drink,
Caught cottaging in Leicester Square, off-guard,
    And the Vice Squad threatening him with the clink
Or (think of Turing) chemical castration,
Ignoring his great service to the nation.

17

What good to say he's known for poetry?
    His early stuff was fine, the later worse.
He drove a taxi for the T. U. C.
    And gave the government a public curse,
But now he is a Grand Old Man and free
    From any obligation to write verse.
He might have been the President of PEN,
Though dying before the age of Wolfenden.

18

Enough of Owen, who at last is free
    Of any obligation to be warmer
Than the grave allows. His immortality
    Is known to the industrious sixth-former,
While every other graduate degree
    Reveals his shameful secrets, like an informer.
This openness leads to a contradiction:
He's now just like a character in fiction.

19

Well, hardly, but familiarity
    Gives us the insights of a necromancer.
The hero's future feels compulsory,
    Predicaments as pointed as a dancer,
And all that happens surely meant-to-be.
    We know each motive like an essay answer.
Just as events could not take place without him,
What happened tells us everything about him.

20

You'll ask, what do we know of Emerald?
    What do we need to know? Only that now
That feared impartial visitor has called,
    Who, though denied, will still call anyhow,
Like a rapacious brigand boat, black-hulled,
    That cuts the innocent waters with its prow
And never stops, for wisdom nor for beauty,
Until it has reached, and caught, and seized its booty.

21

He had some notion of my argument
    About the method of outwitting time.
In fact, he knew exactly what it meant.
    Our cells may well reduplicate, like rhyme,
But they are not precisely equivalent.
    Like transformation in a pantomime
We live in a perpetual disguise.
'It will be someone other than me who dies.'

22

But still, Emerald was superstitious:
    'If I'm a figure in a narrative,
Someone will see my story as fictitious
    And know that I will die, just as I live.
Since even life itself is adventitious,
    No wonder I've misgivings to misgive!
And so the more my life has some coherence,
It may be charged against my disappearance.'

23

'I must aestheticise my ground of being
    And now is the very moment I should start.
I must ignore this wretched body, freeing
    My consciousness to play a better part.
It must be purified, thus guaranteeing
    That I myself become a work of art.
And I'll begin where art and life converge,
In my collections, – and I'll have a purge.'

24

He'd had some charnel trophies, mostly junk,
    Wooden false teeth, and carnival masks inspired
By terminal disease, the skull of a monk
    Trepanned and gilded as a goblet (admired
By Byron) and, in a very well-locked trunk,
    Ampallangs, studs and lip-plates he'd acquired
From Hirschfeld, withered foreskins and a gorgeous
Poison-ring belonging to the Borgias.

25

To rid himself of all this sort of thing
    Felt like an exorcism or giving back
Of all the body's gruesomeness. The King
    Of Sickness and Decay, who turns to black
The putrid colours of his ravaging,
    Might be appeased somehow. The *bric-à-brac*
Was nothing in itself, but was a sign
Of some complicity with the malign.

26

He even came to think he'd been mistaken
    In buying such weird things. It was pure folly!
His confidence in most of art was shaken.
    Someone particularly off his trolley
Was that collector's favourite, Francis Bacon,
    Whose portraits like a melting chocolate lolly
Swallowed their drowning flesh in random brazen
Swirls of paint, round one eye like a raisin.

27

Likewise those tortured souls who give the jitters,
    Who, by not trying, seemed to try the harder:
All the unacknowledged counterfeiters
    Of the genuine, the worshippers of *nada*,
Blank canvases, the squitters and the Schwitters,
    And worst: belated acolytes of Dada
(Who given any kind of rational choice
Would fill their sitting-room with Joseph Beuys?).

Still, the decision gave him some unease.
　　It felt as though he was unloading most
Of his life. The catalogues of Sotheby's,
　　Christie's, Bonhams, went out in the post
To Moscow, Beijing, the Antipodes
　　(And to America, from coast to coast)
And all these bids came flooding in to buy
The soul of Billy. The prices went sky-high.

What did it leave of him? It left the man.
　　Where did it leave him? Cleared of stuff.
What did he think? At least it was a plan.
　　What did he really think? Not quite enough.
The sales were over as soon as they began.
　　They seemed provisional and off-the-cuff,
Yet broke all records with a casual brilliance.
The soul of Emerald made further millions.

You'd think he might have put the proceeds toward a
　　Penance of some kind, perhaps a charity,
To grace his name in this new rage for order,
　　Or simply courted instant popularity
By being lavish where he'd been a hoarder,
　　But now he was sure there was the same vulgarity
In money in itself, and its employment.
He could do nothing with it with enjoyment.

For now the world was feeling really strange.
    His body already ceased to be his friend.
He was a witness to the slow exchange
    Of cells, discomfort he could not transcend,
And pain impossible to rearrange.
    All he could think was, life was going to end.
Not now, of course, not *now*. Not just this minute.
But for this body, yes. And he was in it.

Five

1

We know how the Destroyer lies in wait
 At all the portals of the body, sentry
After sentry bribed to abrogate
 Their sacred duty, and allow him entry.
The total of these entrances is eight
 (An arguable fact, though elementary)
And if the Destroyer finds he can't get in,
He'll always try the less-well-guarded skin.

2

The purses of the kidneys calcified;
 The mouth and nose where breath and eating start,
Free passage to the heaving lung denied,
 And thence to the slowing chambers of the heart;
The anus and the colon, mortified;
 Liver and stomach, put like foes apart;
The eyes and ears, one at a time, or both,
Afflicted with the outrage of a growth.

3

Illness is nothing, unless you believe it so.
 Some trifling thing can grow beyond endurance.
You think if you ignore it, it will grow
 In earnest, and you need some reassurance.
Dash to a specialist, for he will know,
 And he will tell you, – if you have insurance

(His patients never guess he makes his wealth
By proving them already in good health).

4

For most of us are hypochondriacs
    In one form or another: indigestion
Is easily confused with heart attacks;
    Whether a wheeze is cancer or congestion
We're very much in doubt; our lower back's
    A constant problem; but the burning question,
The one that really puts us in ill-humour,
Is whether it's poor posture or a tumour.

5

Frederick Greengage of Harley Street was ready
    To open you up and see. His words, 'I think
We'll have a little look', made you unsteady,
    For he was so much in the gin-and-pink
Himself, a golfing surgeon (good old Freddy!)
    Ready to sink a putt or down a drink,
Reeking of aftershave, a specialist
With body hair that overlapped his wrist.

6

His scrutiny was casual but intensive.
    His fingers only had to touch a gland
To put you all at once on the defensive.
    Although the gesture seemed abrupt, offhand,
It told him everything. He was expensive.
    Much gold was on his hand. The hand was tanned.
He'd cut his thirteenth laminectomy
In time to catch the plane to Chamonix.

7

We miss the signs, or live with them for ages,
  Pretending that they're caused by our neurosis.
Keats was a medic, and he knew the stages
  And all the details of tuberculosis.
Billy knew nothing, save that a pulse presages
  Something or other needing diagnosis
Or regulation (like music going faster
Without the guidance of a concert master).

8

And what it was, he'd simply no idea.
  He knew it in the middle of the night
And lay awake in bed in primal fear,
  But after breakfast he was quite all right.
The symptoms were allowed to disappear.
  The inside of our body's out of sight,
So naturally is quickly out of mind.
He felt in perfect health when he had dined.

9

What do we know? Our system is unplanned.
  Keats understood the bleeding in a cough,
But girls can mistake a foetus for a gland.
  A soldier hit by a Kalashnikov
Can keep on running, though he's lost a hand
  ('Oh, look,' he says, 'my bloody hand's come off').
Your stroke feels like a climax at an orgy.
I had a friend who called his tumour 'Georgie.'

10

Though others had no time to get acquainted
    With their abrupt, final metamorphoses,
Died accidentally, collapsed and fainted,
    Assailed by errant lorries or thromboses,
Never to have their hopes of living tainted,
    Many of my friends received prognoses
Of radical foreshortening, and braved them
(But no one, not even Greengage, could have saved them).

11

Lord Emerald sat in the consulting room
    Stripped to his scarlet pin-striped boxer shorts.
His still-alive cadaver, sunk in gloom,
    Covered in liver-spots and moles and warts,
Seemed almost ready for the family tomb.
    He looked at Greengage and he spoke his thoughts:
'I know you cannot tell, don't get me wrong,
I know you cannot know, but please, . . . how long?'

12

His words trailed off and floated to the ceiling,
    Like futile prayers from an empty pew.
They juddered from his lips and then went reeling
    Like a mis-hit cue ball from a billiard cue.
They touched each polished instrument of healing,
    And left the X-rays in his file askew.
But Greengage, duly wooed, was quite unwon.
He went on writing, and answer came there none.

13

At times like this we are alone, it's true.
    What is unique for us is commonplace.
Nothing that might be said will ever do.
    We are an item in a database,
Faceless as a statistic, through and through
    (Though no one else could claim to have our face),
And at the moment of our death, we know
It is the world, not us, that has to go.

14

For who would tell a baby: 'You've been born!'?
    It's happened. And it happens to everyone.
It's not as though you've climbed the Matterhorn.
    You're simply here. No need to say 'Well done!'
The same with dying. Why should you start to mourn?
    I know it doesn't seem a lot of fun,
That nothingness, but bodies don't seem to hate it.
It comes and goes. So why anticipate it?

15

Later, of course, we're jealous of everything
    That has occurred before our date of birth.
We like to think our own continuing
    Unique experience of Planet Earth
Is of all lives much the most promising.
    We like to think we get our money's worth,
That our enlightenment's beyond compare
(What will come after's neither here nor there).

16

The cavemen thought as much, and so will those
    Who live in caves hereafter (we're content
To live in caves as well as bungalows).
    The past tried hard to be magnificent;
The future may never come to pass, who knows?
    And life itself is just an accident,
A quirk of random consciousness between
Two voids, unmemorable and unseen.

17

Unmemorable only in the sense
    That in the end there will be no one there
To do the remembering, the evidence
    Of our existence leaked into thin air.
There is no play without an audience.
    Nothing's important if no one's there to care.
These are unuseful thoughts, but willy-nilly
They were the ones that now obsessed poor Billy.

18

He took Greengage's silence for a sign
    That in his very being he was cursed
With something so unspeakably malign
    That nothing could be said. He feared the worst.
He'd be content to hear some anodyne
    Assurances, so frequently rehearsed
That no one could believe them, but he would!
He'd clutch at any half-truths if he could.

19

At times like this, when one is really stunned,
    Then superstition weirdly takes a grip:
Public donations to the Tithon Fund,
    Reduced to a trickle from a steady drip,
Like Emerald himself, looked moribund
    Despite the vigour of his sponsorship.
He'd make the millions up himself, and see
If that might purchase immortality!

20

Sick of their wealth, the powerful hope for fame,
    Though what they usually get are curses.
Every philanthropist hopes that his name
    Will live through all the largesse he disburses.
Indifferent poets frequently proclaim
    That they are made immortal by their verses.
It is the hope of every lunatic. It
Is why poor Tithon wanted to be a cricket.

21

And Billy wanted to be like Tithon. The aura
    Of the poem he had rescued for the nation
Breathed over him like 'Nature's sweet restorer
    Balmy sleep.' It was his habitation.
He was himself enamoured of Aurora,
    Who engineered his transubstantiation
Each morning as a cricket on the lawn,
Grateful for daylight, chirping to the dawn.

22

The notion was entirely metaphorical
    As is the case with stories of the gods
And other personages allegorical
    Familiar in the lecture-halls and quads
But striking most of us as unhistorical.
    We tend to deal much more with odds-and-sods,
Whose unexciting lives and their depiction
We find engaging us in works of fiction.

23

But Tithon's tale was not like this at all.
    As Tennyson found out, it was poetic
And melancholic as a garden wall
    (Since melancholy was for him phonetic:
'The woods decay, the woods decay and fall').
    Those dying cadences, so sympathetic,
And then, that image of the whitened pane:
It looks as though he'd Shakespeare on the brain.

24

Had Tennyson, as well as Coleridge, seen
    The Sliphanger Shakespeare manuscripts? Or might
They have been forged? Might Tennyson have been
    Put into them by someone erudite
And devious? So that we read between
    The lines, and somehow believe it at first sight?
Ovid, of course, is there. We would expect it.
Each reference makes sense when we have checked it.

Aurora, Eos, – it is just the same,
    The morning with her streaming diadem
Lightens the deadly night with either name
    And turns the bitterness of four a.m.
Into another day, with sky aflame.
    Dawn is as prompt as any apophthegm.
Who would not hope, in spite of nightly pain,
Who would not hope to sleep, and wake again?

Six

1

Think of the world that Emerald is leaving:
    A world of envied self-aggrandisement,
A world of aspiration and achieving
    Made possible by grave impoverishment,
Where giving is unknown to those receiving
    And half of what's received is fraudulent,
Where the top hundred families are worth
Much more than half the poorest of the earth.

2

Money is something that you can't refuse. It
    Has its uses but it drives a wedge
Between two classes of the men who use it.
    A farmer and a fund both need to hedge.
Workers and brokers each find they can lose it.
    Between the dole queue and the office ledge
Despair may seem to be a common factor, –
But one's the juice and one's the juice extractor.

3

The managers have come into their own.
    They concentrate on totting up the cost
Of paring their investment to the bone
    And milking all the profit. They have lost
All interest in what they manage, thrown
    Away the baby with its water, tossed

The rest into a pot marked 'Dividends'
And shared the proceeds out among their friends.

4

The loyal citizen owns less and less.
    Even the nation's mortgaged to the hilt,
With corporations ready to repossess.
    Greed International, designed and built
To glare down from on high, has no address,
    No conscience, creativity or guilt:
Its blinding towers, each taller than the rest,
Stand in the sun, and darken the oppressed.

5

And what are the issues that obsess the nation?
    A politician ready to amuse.
A singer falling over. Immigration.
    Football. Accents. Royal babies. Shoes.
Social gaffes and sexual speculation.
    Nothing of import gets into the news,
And if it happens to, it will not signify
A thing, unless it's joked about on HIGNFY.

6

Why will there never be a revolution?
    The Church of Greed allows no heretic.
Theories of ownership and distribution
    Sound like the ravings of a lunatic
Within the murmurs of a constitution
    Preferring frequent carrot to crude stick,

The democratic myth of a stale polity
Forever postponing justice and equality.

7

There may be tyrants east of Bucharest
    Who live the golden life, but that's their job,
And they'll use tanks to keep down the oppressed.
    It's subtler here, where we admire a snob
And even want to be one. In the West
    We can't escape the culture of the mob
When money smothers both PM and POTUS,
Who promise titbits to aspiring voters.

8

But now the flowers have all declared for June.
    Their buds split open and their scent emerges,
Luring the drowsy bee to nose and swoon.
    Grasses are taller on the ring-road verges.
Punt poles descend and river-banks are strewn
    With rugs, to satisfy alfresco urges,
While sounds of popping corks greet that late-comer,
The long-expected, popular English summer.

9

Across the country, men in perpetual
    Black tie escort their rigid women to
Trestles of bubbling flutes in pastoral
    Settings: the House of Lords, a private view,
A leg of chicken in an interval
    Of Mozart, anywhere the well-to-do

Might gather in a garden or a terrace
For the showing of some Hockneys, or an heiress.

10

At one of these, designed to celebrate
    The acquisition of the Shakespeare, flocks
Of formal guests began to congregate
    In one of the ancient colleges of Ox-
(Or was it -bridge?) where a prolonged debate
    Had, by Dr Mukhtal Chatterbox
(The tutor there) been finally resolved:
Its authenticity could not be solved.

11

You'd think that a decision of this sort
    Was hardly very useful. Common sense
Is not a critic's port of first resort.
    But scholars like to sit upon the fence,
Holding to scorn what everyone has thought,
    Or else to hold a lengthy conference
At which they can confront, or else appease,
The vanity of their worst enemies.

12

The eager Chatterbox was much like this.
    The truth of the matter was subservient
To his accommodating prejudice
    By holding this gargantuan event
Where all the boffins of analysis
    Could come together with pre-eminent

Shakespeareans and thankfully agree,
Over three days of wine, to disagree.

13

And on the final night, the great and good,
    The interested and uninterested,
Would rush to a reception if they could
    (The RSVPs had been long requested)
To toast whoever it was understood
    Had penned the Tithon sonnets: double breasted
Academicians, the Poet Laureate,
Stratford knights and Ministers of State.

14

Emerald was there; and the miniature
    Countess of Sliphanger, of course; and the
Staff of the Shakespeare Institute; no fewer
    Than seven former Juliets, and three
Hamlets; that scornful TV interviewer;
    The Director-General of the BBC;
The editor of *The Times*; the Prince of Wales;
And undergraduates with green fingernails.

15

His Royal Highness recapitulated
    All the stages of the acquisition
Of the said manuscripts, which vindicated
    Lord Emerald's delicate and lengthy mission
(For which he was to be congratulated).
    The manuscripts themselves, on exhibition,
Looked just as pleased as he was to be there,
Just as expensive, just the worse for wear.

But were they worth it? Were they genuine?
    The Pragger-Wagger making such a fuss,
Surely they were? The showcase they were in
    (Bullet-proof glass, tooled oak and marvellous
Gold fittings, all confirmed their origin)
    Was Chatterbox's stroke of genius.
Like dubious relics in the Vatican,
It was a case of dress maketh the man.

But listen: how do we differentiate
    Between the spurious and the genuine?
The relics we desire, we fabricate:
    The Piltdown Man, that visage from Turin.
Now carbon dating shows they're much too late.
    But we believed in them through thick and thin,
And if a portrait elevates the mind,
Who cares if it's judiciously unsigned?

Who cares if that majestic minuet
    Is by George Handel or by Bononcini?
Or played superbly by a clarinet
    Anachronistically? You'd be a meanie
To say it hadn't been invented yet,
    The sort who'd see a cherry in his Martini
And hold out for an olive. Or decline
A Riesling that wasn't bottled by the Rhine.

19

Who cares if that brown landscape in your attic
    Turns out to be by Roger Van der Weyden?
You never liked it. Though you were ecstatic
    About some wretched portrait, overladen
With blotted ink and idiosyncratic
    Hatchings, possibly by B. R. Haydon
And possibly of Keats, though actually
By and of neither, as far as I can see.

20

And anyway, the genuine might be
    Unarguably second-rate. Who cares
About uncertain authenticity
    When quality will strike you unawares?
Who cares how much you paid? Dishonesty
    Is rife. They say the purchaser bewares,
But if your dealer seems to be asleep
You'll not complain you got your painting cheap.

21

True genius is never false. It makes
    No difference if it sells or doesn't sell.
But forgery is different. All the fakes
    That reach the market, leaked by a cartel
Or by a lonely fool, snapped up by sheiks
    Or badly-advised museums, must do well.
Reichsmarschall Goering certainly paid dear
For his Van Meegerens posing as Vermeer.

Seven

1

Your contract with the world contains no hint
    Of possible escape from superstition.
Here are the idols of belief. They glint
    In twelve-point bold, like prohibition.
Plain common-sense is in the smallest print
    Only to be invoked on one condition:
When hope in lies has failed, and in despair
You don your spectacles, and it is there.

2

So offer me a heaven? I decline.
    It doesn't sound convincing. In some quarters
There may be seven! There isn't one in mine.
    Princess Charlotte baptised in the waters
Of the River Jordan? I'd much prefer the Tyne
    Or Thames or Tees to drench our nation's daughters,
But to what earthly end? It seems to me
Unlikely to bring immortality.

3

Much better a republic in the end
    (Although I know we will not get one soon).
A secular republic I commend,
    With love and peace, society's honeymoon,
Where everyone is everyone else's friend.
    No. It will go down like a lead balloon

(Or one of those revolting steel balloons
Blown out of all proportion by Jeff Koons).

4

My jaw drops deeply when I hear of God
    And all his creatures. Doesn't it seem strange
That all of those who squirm or fly or plod
    Die once and for all? He won't arrange
Eternal heaven for an arthropod,
    But human animals believe they change,
Becoming radiant spirit, leaving behind them
The muddy vestures that had undermined them.

5

Some myths will work if you believe they will:
    Yours may be the single vote that matters
And some young persons are romantics still
    (Though most of them are simply lewd as satyrs).
But those who believe in heaven must be ill
    To go on thinking so, or mad as hatters,
Knowing the delicate organ that affirms
These things burns to a crisp, or crawls with worms.

6

The brain is precious, like the hidden kernel
    Of an ambitious nut inside its shell
Dreaming of being a tree, of the eternal
    Arborial story that it has to tell.
And yet its true existence is diurnal,
    Lofty control-tower of each working cell
Whose mission is elsewhere, to whom it spoke,
Until dislinked, or damaged by a stroke.

7

Let go, let go! The crucial faculties
    Are shutting down, and each to each
Send frantic messages until they freeze,
    The dying operator's urgent speech
Turned nonsense to their teleologies
    In inner galaxies they cannot reach,
As for a time, like voyagers on their own
They hurtle to their destinies, alone.

8

Were any of these things in Emerald's mind
    During the interminable Tithon dinner?
The speeches were so long he felt he'd dined
    Three hours ago. Already he felt thinner
And yes, he'd pondered questions of this kind.
    In thoughts of dying he was no beginner.
He even felt that if the great event
Were to occur just then, he would consent.

9

For after all, it comes at any time.
    Its sense of drama is unorthodox.
You may be searching for a useful rhyme,
    Or eating plums, or putting on your socks,
Or taking children to the pantomime,
    Or listening to Dr Chatterbox.
Aha! That's just what Emerald was doing!
Endless it was (and not a hint of booing).

A perfect time, you'd think, to slip away,
    Especially as Tithon was unable
To, condemned to live another day,
    According to the sonnets' classic fable.
Poetic justice of a kind. Hooray!
    He'd simply cough, and slide beneath the table,
Where waiters would eventually find him
(Leaving his napkin in his place behind him).

But no, you cannot will these things. Besides,
    Billy was scared of dying. He'd prefer
Not to see X-rays of his own insides.
    He could not act as an ambassador
To the court of that great power who decides
    Exactly when your dying will occur.
Which of us could? (The answer is, alas,
Only the lonely heroes of Dignitas.)

Chatterbox was finishing his speech.
    Or was he? Just as tourists lay out towels
Long before breakfast to secure a beach,
    His sentences, with carefully posh vowels,
Laid claim upon the future – his! And each
    Of his pupils present let out hoots like owls
In fond sarcastic joy, and were unable
To stop themselves from thumping on their table.

13

Billy thought Chatterbox an opportunist
    For offering to hold this conference.
He threw out leaden jokes like a balloonist
    Who knows he must rise higher to make sense.
He'd waited like a hired contrabassoonist
    Who only plays the final bars, and hence
Plays them as they've never been heard before,
And has eccentric views about the score.

14

For disagreement is far more exciting
    Than simple truth, and Chatterbox believed
With Donne that truth, however uninviting,
    Requires a lengthy struggle to be achieved.
But not by him. He didn't do much writing.
    He spoke in lengthy paragraphs, looked peeved,
And much as ladies used to hold salons,
He liked to edit work by other dons.

15

Since Billy had been praised and made his own
    Response, the evening could go on without him.
He thought the whole occasion too high-flown.
    He couldn't recall the things they said about him,
And all the facts recounted were well-known,
    While Chatterbox's views (well, who could doubt him?)
Were piling up and anxious to arrive,
Like Sunday traffic on the M25.

16

Just then a face leaned forward into view
    Much as it might if suddenly engrossed
In what was being said, and then withdrew,
    Dim at the far end of the table, most
Like a mask, or someone playing peekaboo,
    Unwelcome to Emerald as Banquo's ghost.
A sight he could not easily dismiss:
The face was Greengage's, his nemesis!

17

Emerald hadn't noticed it before
    Among the profiles of the guests, in layers
Along the full length of the table, nor
    At the earlier reception, where the players
Spoke their opening lines. And furthermore,
    Like that mysterious diner at Emmaus,
It owned a surprising superfluity
That gave it an unearthly perspicuity.

18

And there it was again! It looked directly
    Down the long table at poor Emerald
Who in his turn found himself circumspectly
    Looking back at it. He was appalled.
Was he quite certain he had seen correctly?
    And what exactly was it he beheld?
A pair of eyes with an accusing stare
Beneath a quantity of eyebrow hair.

19

They seemed to say, what, are you still alive?
    They seemed to say, you, is it you? I well
Remember thinking that you'd not survive.
    I'm here to warn you further. Can't you tell?
It's now inevitable, that high dive
    Into the one-way street, the terminal,
The bleakness of a fruitless consultation,
The body's final insubordination.

20

Just one more superstition for poor Billy:
    Not every doctor is omniscient,
And that fixed stare might mean that too much chilli
    Required his concentration to prevent
Digestive turbulence from willy-nilly
    Turning into an audible event
(Frightfully infra dig to eructate
Amidst the speeches and the college plate).

21

Who knows if this were true or not? Or if
    Greengage had even noticed him? The light
Was dark as Rembrandts. Look at his handkerchief
    Trying to keep his mouth concealed. He might
Have neatly turned his belch into a sniff,
    Disguising an unguilty appetite
Ready to down five courses, plus libations,
After dismembering a dozen patients.

22

And why was Greengage there in any case?
    Could it have been an entente cordiale?
Surgery and verse come face to face
    As if to boost the college's morale?
No, it was something much more commonplace:
    Greengage was brother of the Principal
And liked to visit him, because (with prudence)
It let him chat up all the clean-limbed students.

23

The outcome of superstitions is a flight.
    Reason dissolves into a panicked blur.
If circumstances tell you to sit tight
    And deal with them, somehow you'd still prefer
A change of scene to putting up a fight,
    As though a facile trust in distance were
A way to make them disappear (much sadder
Than never walking underneath a ladder).

24

And so it was with Billy. He supposed
    That stare from Greengage ('What, are you still alive?')
To mean, though nothing had been diagnosed,
    That he'd not thought that Billy would survive.
Well, Billy would survive! And he proposed,
    With all the insouciance he could contrive,
A visit to his eldest son in Rome,
The closest thing for him to going home.

Eight

1

Home is not one place. Home is where you yield
    Your being up to someone else, and know
That you'll be taken care of, loved, and healed.
    Home is simply where you have to go.
Even Brooke's 'corner of a foreign field'
    Became a home of sorts, and goes to show
That when your life's a mess, maternal earth
Is home as much as the Rugby of your birth.

2

He was the Byron of his time, alive
    And restless. And it's hardly strange to find
That sex and war were things that made both thrive
    (Although the second largely in the mind).
Think of them as swimmers poised to dive
    Into experience, then undermined.
Both could, and did, display a giant erection.
Both were defeated by a chance infection.

3

From Missolonghi to Trebuki Bay
    The blithe Destroyer struck these poets down
With various kinds of premature decay:
    Lanced and bled, livid, fevered, brown,
Their bodies fought, and yet by break of day
    Neither was still a person, but a noun,

Simply the letters that made up his name,
The trademark of his poems, and his fame.

    4

(Yet home is also always where you set
    Out from, of every radius the centre.
Sometimes it is a place that you forget,
    Or it's unreal, and you are its inventor,
And life itself is a consuming debt.
    Not an adventure, then, but an abventure,
A path of chance, perhaps a rigmarole,
But rather a long haunting than a goal.)

    5

When life is nothing but a molecule
    And then a blastocyst, and then begins
Its staggering journey, pushing a milking stool
    Across the kitchen floor; learning that grins
Accomplish more than howling; going to school;
    It's always mindful of its origins.
The future is an unknown destination,
The past a powerful impulse of causation.

    6

Home's the safe ground beneath a somersault.
    Home is an intuition in the genes.
In any variation, home's the default
    Position. Home is forgiveness, and it means
That nothing's ever really all your fault.
    And when the world's displeasure intervenes
In your best hopes, or shows its unconcern,
Home is the place to which you can return.

7

If earth is Mother, so a son may be,
    Or else a father to a father, tender
To the frail being in his custody,
    The mirror of his soul and of his gender,
The genuine and easy company
    To whom his coming is a mute surrender.
For Billy it felt the strangest of all claims
To think of going to stay with his son James.

8

Home in this case was an extensive flat
    That James had purchased on the Aventine
When first appointed as a diplomat.
    Its terrace overlooked a Roman pine.
His boyfriend was an Italian pussycat
    Who knew about Italian design:
Ettore Sottsass bookcases, a sofa
By Maranello, and Gucci chauffeur.

9

Their parties featured in the Sunday papers
    With photographs, part-secular, part-holy,
Of racing-drivers and opinion-shapers,
    A Cardinal and Angelina Jolie
Performing (willingly) four-handed capers
    Upon a baby grand by Fazioli,
With, in the corners, alternative duets
And other *tête-à-têtes* that time forgets.

Children are parents if they have to be,
    The bigger sister hoisting up the toddler.
Their love is large in reciprocity:
    The mollycoddled is a mollycoddler.
Love's earliest model is the family.
    The model child becomes the modeller
Of tolerant relationships, – forbearance,
Care and nurture, all learned from the parents.

Quite so, but what about the smaller brother?
    He finds that he is loved by everyone,
Who in their turn of course love one another.
    Where is *his* object? Suppose he's an only son?
It may be that he'll only love his mother,
    And in the end, when all is said and done,
He'll play that role, from which no one recovers,
Of being himself a mother to his lovers.

Since James had lost his father as a child
    (His mother told him he must keep his distance),
It had been diffy to be reconciled,
    But they had long contrived a co-existence:
When Billy phoned him up in fear, James smiled
    And simply took the line of least resistance.
'Dad, there's a room for you. There always is.
So don't apologise. Just turn up. Please!'

So James and Alessandro talked to him
    For hours, until he lost all inhibition.
They hovered round him like the cherubim
    Above an Agony. It was their mission
To fill up his Campari to the brim
    And listen to his tales of the physician
From whom he'd fled, in his desire to live
And find some miracle alternative.

14

And James was old enough as never before
    To find his father's presence commonplace
(No more divided loyalties), therefore
    Unchallenging. At forty, he could face
The simple claims of someone near fourscore
    Without embarrassment, in male embrace.
It was a relationship in disrepair,
And, after all, he had some love to spare.

15

So Alessandro leaped up from his chrome-
    And-hide armchair to go and make ambitious
Suppers for them. He was a gastronome
    As well as a kept boy. He thought his dishes
Would make dear James's father feel at home,
    And he was quite correct. They were delicious.
He could whip eggs and cream and ham, and coax
Them into a love affair with artichokes.

16

A dying man may look at a banana
    Or touch a little salad with his fork.
He may not feel like tackling a sultana
    Sponge or stir-fried greens with char siu pork,
And may not put a match to his Havana.
    He won't take joy in hearing a pulled cork.
His body's guarding what it has, quite sure
It hasn't got the appetite for more.

17

Try him with griddled rib-eye steak and sticky
    Toffee pud: he'll push his plate away.
At any buffet he'll be more than picky.
    He hopes a junket will be curds-and-whey.
The spirit's willing, though. It can be tricky,
    And Alessandro's artichoke soufflé
Was so enticing that it once was said
That it could raise a gourmet from the dead.

18

It certainly raised Billy's spirits. He
    Considered Rome to be a better place,
The place where everyone would like to be,
    Than all those where he had to show his face
And be Lord Emerald. Here he felt free,
    And fallen off the Destroyer's database.
For a moment, then, though near his eightieth,
A missing person in the realm of death.

19

We all have tickets for the Great Event,
    Paid in advance and non-transferable.
You'll go, however inconvenient,
    However demanding or unusual.
No one will ask you later how it went,
    No one to murmur: 'Was it terrible?'
No one to sit up with you half the night,
To stroke your hair, and say: 'It's quite all right!'

20

It will not be an entry in your diary.
    It will not be an item in the news
About which you can make your own inquiry.
    You'll never read the excellent reviews.
Your ticket has no date-stamp of expiry.
    It is a present that you can't refuse.
You have it for a lifetime, what is worse,
Dog-eared in your wallet or your purse.

21

You will not like the thing one little bit.
    You know the outcome and you know the theme.
You know the part you have to play in it.
    It may not do much for your self-esteem,
But you've the starring role, you must admit.
    You mustn't rubbish the production team.
They're working to designs of their employer,
Who is the mastermind, and the Destroyer.

22

Yes, he is always there. You will have met him,
    Like Billy, in your mirror, in the night.
He'll be inside your head if you will let him.
    Once you have thought of him, he's there all right.
It isn't very easy to forget him,
    Though there are moments when you think you might:
Prosecco, chilled, at six; soufflé at nine;
A morning's walk upon the Aventine.

23

After breakfast, Billy was inclined
    To go out by himself into the pretty
Parco di Savello. He could find
    A panorama of the misty city
There like no other. It was of a kind
    To lift the heart and to dispel self-pity.
There, grey to the left, St Peter's Dome,
And then the rooftops of the rest of Rome.

24

His favourite place for quiet meditation
    Was a basilica – Santa Sabina,
Fifth century, a modern restoration.
    Nothing could be severer or serener.
From there he wandered to the Metro station,
    The Circo Massimo, where Messalina
Urged on her favourite charioteers, and now
The dogs and tourists wander anyhow.

25

He bought gelato, as a child would do,
    And rode beneath the ground to Barberini,
To visit the Palazzo and walk through
    The galleries of Sienese bambini
Who writhed on their Madonnas' laps, and who
    Looked more like portly men with bloated greeny
Skin and bored expressions, more like Billy
In fact, than Christ-with-Linnet, or with-Lily.

26

But then he came to Caravaggio
    And his precise expression of a myth.
Poor Holofernes' lips a tortured O,
    His neck near-severed. Leaning back, Judith
In some distaste, frowning a little as though
    Learning a difficult piano part, and with
Her woman standing grimly by the bed,
Holding a sack in which to keep the head.

27

And the myth? In all its solemn mystery
    It kept its riddle close. But what it meant
Was something to do with masculinity,
    That challenges either through being impudent
Or inaccessible. The woman's free
    Of it by rendering it impotent.
Salomé, Judith, – theirs a macabre wedding
Of opposites, achieved by a beheading.

28

Was this what Judy would have liked to do?
    Something about that stern fastidiousness
Reminded him of her, how she'd subdue
    The clay with either fist, make it confess
To features like a Golem. He thought he knew
    Why she had stiffened under his caress
And needled him to say what he could not say,
And gave more passion to the lifeless clay.

29

He set off back along the Via del
    Quirinale, and admired the beauty
Of Sant' Andrea, like a golden bell
    Scattered with Bernini's marble putti,
Startlingly white and tumbling there pell-mell.
    (Some think Bernini overdone and fruity,
But nowadays it isn't done to mock
The sensuous ecstasies of the baroque.)

30

A moment just to rest his legs beside
    Carlo Alberto of Savoy, in bronze,
And wearing an enormous hat, astride
    His horse, leading his absent echelons
Through the Giardini. Billy sighed,
    His muscles ticking like automatons.
The bench rose through his body like a vice.
His eyes were swimming, and his cheeks were ice.

31

He said: 'I'll feel much better in a while.
    It's silly to have been walking half the day.'
Who did he say it to? A silent pile
    Of stone and greenish metal on display!
Carlo Alberto did not respond or smile.
    Carlo Alberto had nothing at all to say.
Carlo Alberto, like every equestrian statue,
Stared straight ahead, with one hoof lifted at you.

32

And Billy did not feel much better. There,
    Coming towards him, talking fortissimo
Between Italian colleagues, debonair
    And tanned, was Greengage, with a portfolio!
What was *he* doing here in Rome? Was he aware
    Of Billy? Coming to save him, perhaps? Although
The scene turned like a kaleidoscope before him,
Billy was absolutely sure he saw him.

33

And that was all, or rather the last he saw
    Of anything. And was it a mirage?
Who knows? They say that sometimes just before
    We die, like batteries trying to recharge,
Our brains rush back through life, breaking the door
    Down in one last effort to enlarge
Experience before the final breath.
So there was Greengage in the shape of death.

34

Do you believe in ghosts? No, nor do I.
    Nor in involuntary transportation.
If it were truly Greengage there, then why?
    A lecture at some medical foundation?
A holiday perhaps (it *was* July)?
    And if it were, is that the explanation
Of Billy's dying at that moment, seeing from
Across the park the man that he was fleeing from?

Nine

1

What is it like, this business of expiring?
    We'll never know, at least until we do it.
It's usually a matter of blown wiring
    Or struggling to breathe. Let's not pursue it.
I find the subject really uninspiring,
    Even though you and I must each go through it.
I couldn't, even if I wanted to,
Explain how Emerald became napoo.

2

Or if, or how, his soul pursued its quest
    For further life. Was it like when one pees
After some great constriction, half-distressed,
    And the groin relaxes suddenly to give one ease
And it feels as though one has been strangely blest
    As the long shiver goes out through the knees?
Or was it like the thudding at the chest
Of a living corpse, too early put to rest?

3

Better to simply wait to fall asleep,
    When the day dies, and will not rise again.
Or not for you. The little creatures creep
    About the garden. Like a specimen,
The moon is stained upon the night, and deep
    Your fellow mortals sleep. And then

They wake, and go about their own affairs.
You have no interest in yours. Or theirs.

4

Aurora wakes them, with her lover's touch.
     She wakes the careless and the foolish, those
Who are greedy for the opening day, and such
     As squander it, those whom the goddess chose,
Who never claimed to prize her overmuch,
     And those whose inclination is to doze
Through a long life progressively diminished
And then to be resentful when it's finished.

5

You leave your uncompleted story pending.
     There'll be a 'Catch Up Here', no 'Now Read On.'
The soul is always searching for an ending-
     Beyond-the-ending, to cheat oblivion.
But no, it isn't any good pretending.
     You are your body. What is gone is gone.
And that is why it's such a painful wrench,
Like Billy Emerald on his Roman bench.

6

Enough. It happened. As it had to do.
     But in his changing of one cityscape
For one not different enough, it's true
     That he changed nothing. He could not reshape
His life. Or make it longer. Death was due.
     It makes you think of that famous failed escape

In the story of the appointment in Samarra
(No, not that brilliant novel by John O'Hara).

7

I mean that fable of eastern origin
    About avoiding death, that in the form
We know it is most commonly found in
    Sheppey, a play by W. Somerset Maugham,
An unread writer who could really spin
    A story, keep you guessing, and rewarm
An ancient tale to underline the climax
(Without the aid of Google or of iMacs).

8

Once there was a merchant of Baghdad
    Who needed market-stuffs, so sent along
His servant. After a little while, the lad
    Returned in fear. He said: 'While in the throng
A woman jostled me. I turned. She made
    A threatening gesture, as if to do me wrong.
I saw that it was Death! Lend me your horse
To leave this city!' The merchant said: 'of course.'

9

The servant dug his spurs in. Off he went
    To distant Samarra to avoid his fate.
The merchant went to the market where he'd sent
    The servant, and saw me standing at the gate.
'Why,' he said, 'did you make that violent
    Gesture to him this morning?' 'I have a date

With him soon in Samarra. He's my prize,'
I said. 'No violent gesture. Pure surprise.'

10

That was Death talking, which he does not often
    Do, nor often as a woman, either.
But female tones will not do much to soften
    The essential message of that lean old scyther
Which, if he's speaking to you, means a coffin.
    The choice is male or female. I'll have neither.
He can keep quiet, this side of the tomb,
Button his lipless mouth, say nought, keep stumm.

11

The forecast stoppages have cancelled travel
    On many of the customary routes.
There is no settling of the long disputes
    As all the spendthrift maps of blood unravel.
The drivers stall. There are no substitutes.
    The ghosts of oceans whisper in the gravel
And it is much too late now to postpone
The last ungrateful stillness of the bone.

12

Fingers that fondled at the collar-bone
    To reach a button or a favourite locket,
Or interlinked with others, or alone
    Reached down a polished thigh to find a pocket,
Or clasped behind a supine skull, or, prone,
    Spread in the earth, straining a shoulder socket,
Are now disjointed. How long they have waited
For joy, and now are disarticulated!

13

Folded across the chest in attitudes
    Of resignation or of blank repose
(Or formal pudeur in the case of nudes),
    The arms are cross-bones now, and so compose
One of those symbols of our fearful moods
    Beneath a head with darkness for a nose
And eyes that once were radiant aureoles
For love's long purposes, now merely holes.

14

Toes that were lifted on themselves to dance
    Have fallen now. The jig, the tarantella,
Even the grave pavane, have now no chance.
    The lightly dimpled knee is a patella,
And where were breasts is insignificance,
    The reaching ribs collapsed like an umbrella.
The muscles and the skin have now all gone,
In deference to the lingering skeleton.

15

Why is it hideous, admonitory?
    It's what remains as our remains, its clicks
And jabbering our own memento mori.
    We may enumerate arithmetic's
Amazingly consistent inventory:
    Our bones amount to just 206,
Yet when we count them we feel slightly cheated.
It's like a puzzle that has been completed.

16

And yes, it is complete, this lifeless thing,
   Exposed and useless. Yet it terrifies.
You know it's just a kind of scaffolding.
   It might have been your friend. It's just his size.
But it's an absence, and it's sickening.
   He's there and not there, worse than a disguise.
That's why we burn it (or, more orthodox,
Screw it down tightly in a buried box).

17

So what else might we do with it? For us
   The notion of its being vertical
Is either hideous or humorous.
   What's more, not even all of it's original.
'Granny, how old are you?' I used to fuss.
   Her answer oddly invoked the skeletal
To make me see the bones growing beneath:
'Old as my tongue, but older than my teeth.'

18

Granny, the first dead person that I saw,
   Or rather, the first dead person that I knew.
(I do not count the mother, years before,
   Flattened upon Blackheath by a V-2.
I didn't come up close to her, therefore
   Her death seemed theoretical.) But who
Could have prepared me for Granny's motionless
And strangely tiny face, its yellowness?

19

There's nothing left of her that I can see
    Except these moments I remember, old
In themselves, and rarer as I atrophy,
    Dying with me, of course, if they're untold.
Not like the Malagasy's scrutiny
    And handling of the bones themselves, unrolled
From lambas, like carpets for spring-cleaning, spread
With tenderness, in their village of the dead.

20

Like disarticulated alphabet
    They are not bodies but entanglements.
Their place of burial, like a badger's sett
    Is found beneath their painted monuments--
A palisade, a wooden minaret
    Crusted with funerary ornaments--
From which the devoted Malagasy garner
Familiar remnants in their Famadihana.

21

They are quite practical, where we sing psalms.
    The Famadihana is a ritual
Of homage and affection, legs and arms
    Sorted like vegetables, farcical
Pieces like kneecaps, heads that have lost their charms
    Stroked for the memory of their animal
Movements and their smiling countenances,
Their downcast moods, their anguish, their quick glances.

The skull speaks nothing of its history
    And nothing it can do will make it change.
It stares for ever with no memory,
    Nothing to justify or rearrange.
It has no knowledge of futurity.
    The world it visited is now so strange,
So inaccessible in all its starkness,
It could not be reflected in that darkness.

23

The skull is like a mask. The emptiness
    Of eyes and nose is a triangulation
Locating emotion in complete undress.
    The mask is a carnival of alienation
Where the impersonal, with great finesse,
    Longs to be found out for impersonation.
The mask is half in love with its unmasker
Like the dead families of Madagascar.

24

But there's another similar scenario
    Commemorating the Destroyer's hand.
He as an aesthete and grand impresario
    Greatly encouraged what his minions planned:
The grisly chambers in the Cripta Ossario
    Of the Frati Cappuccini in Rome, a band
Of brothers who could rival Montezuma
In amassing bodies with a sense of humour.

You might go there yourself, as Billy went,
　　To see the bones. It's long been a museum.
It may not seem quite as magnificent
　　As the Arch of Trajan or the Colosseum,
Or lift the spirit like the sacrament
　　Taken with Pergolesi's last Te Deum
In chords voluptuous and fortissimo
Beneath that ceiling by Michelangelo.

You'll find it in the Via de Veneto.
　　That street where in the 'fifties students met
To prove they'd heard of Gramsci and Pareto
　　(Or see Anita Ekberg's silhouette)
When Mastroianni was a hot potato
　　And you could hear the Modern Jazz Quartet.
In early spring the heavy orange trees
Glow like the fruit of the Hesperides.

The traffic's heavier now, but still that crypt
　　Lies deep in musty silence, where the friars
Have gathered all the unfleshed parts and clipped
　　Them up in shapes of fans and flowers with wires
Like doodling in an ancient manuscript,
　　As if to save them from eternal fires,
Transforming human souls into cave-dwellers,
Disguised as holy symbols in their cellars.

Pelvises splayed like blossoms; skulls in lines,
    Temple by temple, ignorant of ears;
Femurs laid down like vintages of wines;
    Digits like crystal dripping from chandeliers;
Basket work of rib-cage; clusters of spines;
    Altars of patellas stacked in tiers;
Stars made of toes and jaws in asterisks;
Spirals of discs and bony obelisks.

And if you visit them, you may, like Billy,
    Find that the skeletal is doctrinaire,
The message, like the crypt itself, too chilly
    For any counsel other than despair.
But death is democratic. Willy-nilly
    The bones are counselling courage. They declare:
'Look upon us circumspectly. We
Were once like you; and like us you will be.'

A little scamp giggled at the displays
    And thought them toys not tombs. Her fingers slipped
Out of her father's as she ran the maze
    Of clammy cellars that made up the crypt,
Unknowing of those not-too-distant days
    When her slight body would become full-hipped,
Her pelvis ready to cradle and deliver
Her own slight current of the human river.

If we could send our life away by FedEx,
    Poste-restante to a heaven of our choice;
If we could truly trust our life to medics
    And only lose it as we lose our voice;
If we could take a pill for death (like headaches)
    On permanent prescription, we'd rejoice.
We'd treat it as no more than indigestion.
To be or not to be would be no question.

Ten

1

When does a poem end? There is no prize
    For breasting some established tape, no clock
That strikes when time is up. Novels comprise
    The total of what we need to know, their stock
Is counted when the hero weds or dies.
    Poems are open-ended, more ad hoc.
(Who is to say that this extravaganza
Couldn't put up with just another stanza?)

2

Yet while the notebook fills and the world spins,
    Time has something to say about the matter.
Though cognisant of when a thing begins
    And when it ends, it can't foretell the latter.
And equally, it can't run widdershins
    Back through all the scribble and the chatter.
Time, like its victims, is as ignorant
Of where things come from as of where they went.

3

So don't consult your watch or calendar
    To tell you when a poem's run its course.
A poem's manifold but singular,
    A tower of strength if not a tour de force.
When free of you, it is your avatar,
    Your map of thought, your memory's resource,

Your consciousness, your neurons' rich notation,
A cycle of completed cogitation.

4

I took another journey, not north-east
    This time. The south-west seemed the way to go.
The car was packed. The summer had not ceased
    And gave no sign of ever doing so.
We followed it to France. But first a feast
    At Wickham, close to Portsmouth. Then the slow
Movement of the harbour lights, the ferry
Just for a moment feeling stationary.

5

The shipping lanes were blinking in the dawn.
    Each buoy, unknown to us, had its own name,
The waters of the Channel calm as corn,
    The waves of water and of wind the same.
Travel by water is like being born
    (Or dying, because we go the way we came).
We travel as if there's something we have to prove.
To stay alive we must be on the move.

6

I have another ear-worm in my head.
    It's there in the Channel, under the evening star.
I hear it before I know it, going to bed.
    It's Poulenc's music for *L'Histoire de Babar*,
The part where the elephant is crowned and wed,
    Rich modulations, most spectacular,
Written with more than a friendly nod, I'll wager,
To Chopin's melting Prelude in F Sharp Major.

7

It's just the thing that Poulenc liked to do:
    A tea-shop waltz, a hymn, a jour de fête,
The Little Old Lady's kindness as a cue
    For something from *Apollon Musagète*
(Stravinsky wouldn't mind that – if he knew).
    A little Mozart with a cigarette?
Why not? The shade of Haydn for a Presto?
It's almost a post-modern manifesto.

8

But here's the pachydermic coronation.
    It lifts the soul, though not a note is sounded.
The chorded grace-notes lend a strange vibration
    To a majestic melody that's grounded
As much in sorrow as in jubilation.
    It's in my brain. I'm smothered and surrounded
By everything that Poulenc put across.
About his childhood, and maternal loss.

9

We drove through miles and miles of rural France,
    With plane trees, beautiful blonde cows, and castles.
Regions reflected its uncertain governance.
    Here bales of hay like lost post-office parcels,
There blackened sunflowers in silent dance,
    Or maize in crispened sheaths and feathery tassels.
Landscape like language is the practice of
The people and the kind of food they love.

Travel reminds you of the life that settles
    In a valley. The forests barely cleared. Strict rows
Of vines. Geranium villages with petals
    Fallen on cobbles like a bleeding nose.
Bucket railways ferrying ore for metals,
    The enterprise that goes where the river goes,
And the river with its stubborn energy
And memory goes only to the sea.

Unlike a river, the car begins to climb
    To chalky uplands, where the tormentil
And butterfly proclaim the summertime,
    And then twists down again, hill after hill,
To the region of the lemon and the lime,
    Where the sun shines upon, and always will,
The pink and salmon villas in their pines.
The cypresses, gold bream, and rosy wines.

At midday in a bar, upon my knee
    A mustard-coloured caterpillar, sparse
As a dental brush, with stripes of red, feels free
    To hunch itself along (as bold as brass)
My thigh, thinking, no doubt, I am a tree
    Where it can change into its alias,
A creature that might fly for a day or two,
A fragile metamorphosed ingénue.

13

How strange the things that make us feel remorse!
    I cannot be its wished environment,
So try some coaxing to divert its course
    From its preferred and trousered gradient
On to a folded map. It won't. So force
    Is necessary, mild admonishment
And gentle nudging from my fingertip.
But still the creature cannot get a grip.

14

I feel a passion for this writhing shred
    Of bristle, haunted by its blind intent.
I cannot wait to see it fly. Instead
    I must be witness to a banishment.
I wouldn't want to see it hurt or dead.
    But it is gone. I didn't see where it went.
Fallen upon a bush, perhaps? A brief
Moment of recomposure on a leaf?

15

Our lives are hardly richer or more varied,
    No less determined and no more achieved.
Although a butterfly is never married
    Or has a family, or is bereaved,
Believes in anything, is ill, or buried,
    You cannot say its life is misconceived.
Perhaps we'd like such radical existence,
Pure carelessness, pure flight, and pure persistence.

16

And now the French have started a new term.
　　Political scandals rehearse a comedy
Whose headlines promise they will make you squirm.
　　I saw an ancient man being helped into the sea
(For the beaches now belong to the infirm),
　　Pitied him, but thought it might be me.
His daughter launched him like a coracle.
His smile was bullish, brave and whimsical.

17

So life continues for a little while.
　　The wine is going, but we keep the cork.
And we imagine saying with a smile:
　　'Ah, yes, that was the summer I could walk.'
(Ruefully but with a certain style)
　　And then: 'That was the winter I could talk.'
The score still sings, but faculties agree
To leave, like Haydn's Farewell Symphony.

18

One by one, they tip-toe and depart.
　　No excuses, and no explanations.
The brain remembers clearly how the heart
　　Used to conduct those brilliant orchestrations.
It falters now, unlikely to restart.
　　No forward tempo, and no consolations.
Mere memory of music, undiminished,
Surges in silent bliss, till it is finished.

19

To die with music in your head would be
    The thing. While prepping up your favourite
Supper for two, a gilt-head bream, maybe.
    The smell of kitchens is the opposite
Of the smell of hospitals, though what you see
    In them has similarities: a bit
Of knife-work, blood, and laying-out will take a
Corpse along the way to meet its maker.

20

How does the poem end? In the assertion
    That every day's no better than it gets
And nothing brighter than a mild diversion
    (A Mate-in-Three, a Beaune, a track by Getz)
Is likely to occur until the insertion
    Of your own pelvis in those bone rosettes?
I hope not. And anyway, hope is the thing.
For life, though finite, is a continuing.

21

To think of friends my age, some of them older
    But many younger. Now all dead. They come
To mind with Death already at their shoulder
    As though I knew them to be fated. Some
Were unprepared. They felt the room grow colder.
    Others were ready for long martyrdom.
This knowledge is our burden. Though without it
We'd never have the chance to think about it.

So this is how the poem ends. It says
    You have to tolerate outrageousness
Without outrage. The disappearances
    Of those you knew and loved and learned to bless
Will hurt far more than yours. Your premises
    Foreclose according to the lease. And yes,
This final shot is how the poem ends:
The Destroyer taking selfies with my friends.

The moon is rising, pale above the pines.
    My hand is moving on the page at leisure
Beside a flickering light. It makes these lines.
    I write about writing them, a kind of Escher.
The poem is a string of chosen signs.
    Above, my hand maintains its gentle pressure,
Guiding the drying ink. The page lies under,
And as I write I look at it in wonder.

Lucent the points of burning air. To sit
    On terraces is to not want to go
So long as the flames glow. No, not one bit.
    Reluctance is a struggle: burning slow,
Or hoping to be suddenly relit
    Like those renewing birthday candles. Though
Birthdays have been and gone, and few will come
Again, still, think of this: there may be some.